Watching the Weather

By Edana Eckart

Children's Press®
A Division of Scholastic Inc.
New York / Toronto / London / Auckland / Sydney
Mexico City / New Delhi / Hong Kong
Danbury, Connecticut

Photo Credits: Cover © Steve Bloom/Getty Images; p. 5 © Luc Beziat/Getty Images; p. 7 © Alan R. Moller/Getty Images; p. 9 © Phil Schermeister/National Geographic Image Collection; p. 11 © Timothy Shonnard/Getty Images; p. 13 © Raymond Gehman//National Geographic Image Collection; p. 15 © Samurai Wildlife Prods. Int/Getty Images; p. 17 © Getty Images; p. 19 © Kim Steele/Photodisc/Getty Images; p. 21 © Rudi Von Briel/PhotoEdit Inc.
Contributing Editors: Shira Laskin and Jennifer Silate
Book Design: Michelle Innes

Library of Congress Cataloging-in-Publication Data

Eckart, Edana.
    Watching the weather / by Edana Eckart.
    p. cm. — (Watching nature)
    Summary: A simple introduction to how weather changes and how
    meteorologists forecast the weather.
    Includes bibliographical references and index.
    ISBN 0-516-27601-8 (lib. bdg.) — ISBN 0-516-25940-7 (pbk.)
    1. Weather—Juvenile literature. [1. Weather.] I. Title. II. Series.

QC981.3.E25 2004
551.6—dc22

                                                        2003014451

Contents

1 Warm Weather   4

2 A Storm   8

3 Studying Weather   18

4 New Words   22

5 To Find Out More   23

6 Index   24

7 About the Author   24

Today, the **weather** is warm.

The Sun is bright.

5

Look at the sky.

The weather is **changing**.

Dark clouds are moving above us.

They block the Sun.

There will be a **storm** soon.

The dark clouds bring rain.

The wind blows, too.

There is **lightning** during the storm.

13

After the storm, the sky clears.

We can see the Sun again.

The air is cooler after
the storm.

The weather has changed.

Some people **study** the weather.

They look at **special** pictures that show how the clouds are moving.

People who study the weather are on the **news**.

They tell us what the weather will be like tomorrow.

The weather is fun to watch.

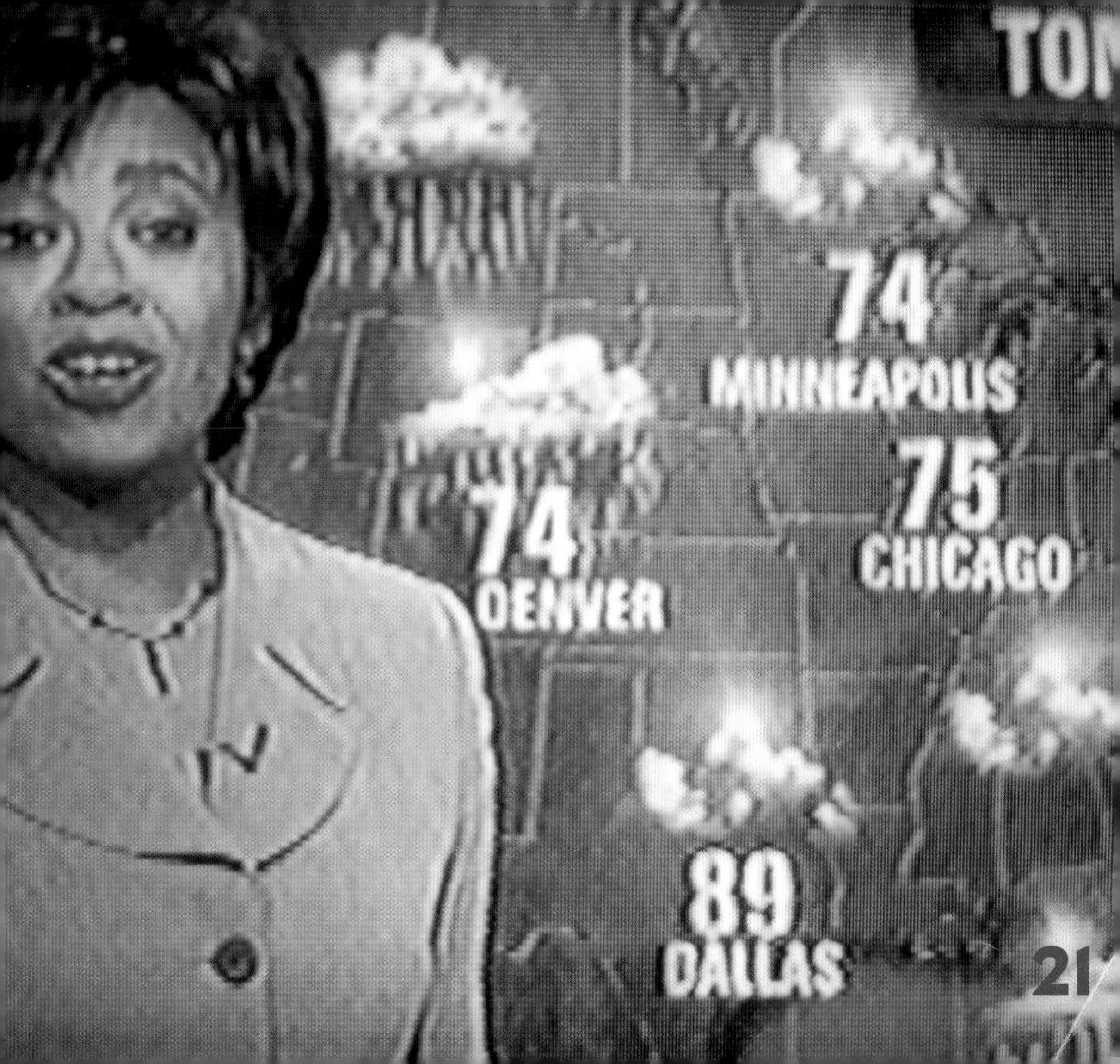
74
MINNEAPOLIS
75
CHICAGO
74
DENVER
89
DALLAS

New Words

changing (**chaynj**-ing) becoming different from
    the way it was before

lightning (**lite**-ning) a thin, bright light you see in
    the sky during some storms

news (**nooz**) a show on television or the radio that
    tells you about things that have just happened

special (**spesh**-uhl) something that is different in
    a good way from what is usual

storm (**storm**) weather with snow or rain and
    a lot of wind

study (**stuhd**-ee) to work at learning things by
    reading books and thinking

weather (**weth**-uhr) how hot or cold it is outside
    and what it is like outside in other ways

To Find Out More

Books
Weather
by Seymour Simon
HarperCollins Children's Book Group

Weather Words and What They Mean
by Gail Gibbons
Holiday House, Incorporated

Web Site
Sky Diary: Kidstorm
http://www.skydiary.com/kids/
This Web site has lots of information about the weather including storms, lightning, tornadoes, and hurricanes.

Index

changing, 6, 16

clouds, 8, 10, 18

lightning, 12

news, 20

rain, 10

special, 18

storm, 8, 12, 14, 16

study, 18, 20

Sun, 4, 8, 14

weather, 4, 6, 16, 18, 20

wind, 10

About the Author

Edana Eckart has written several children's books. She enjoys bike riding with her family.

Reading Consultants

Kris Flynn, Coordinator, Small School District Literacy, The San Diego County Office of Education

Shelly Forys, Certified Reading Recovery Specialist, W.J. Zahnow Elementary School, Waterloo, IL

Paulette Mansell, Certified Reading Recovery Specialist, and Early Literacy Consultant, TX